Akbar and Birbal

Stories of Wit and Humour

Komal Mehra

Contents

1.	How Akbar and Birbal Met	3
2.	Mahesh Das and the Sentry	5
3.	A Matter of Crows	8
4.	Length of the Stick	10
5.	Half-light, Half-shadow	12
6.	Who is the Greater Fool?	15
7.	The Most Beautiful Child	18
8.	The Punishment	22
9.	Begum and Birbal	25
10.	Those Who Cannot See	30

STERLING PRESS PRIVATE LIMITED

1
How Akbar and Birbal Met

Emperor Akbar was very fond of hunting. Even as a child, he would leave his lessons and tutors and go for riding and hunting. When he grew up, he was a better rider and a more fearless hunter than any of his courtiers.

One day, Akbar and his men were chasing a tiger. Akbar and a few brave soldiers rode so fast that they left all the others behind. They had travelled a long distance from the royal capital of Agra, and as the sun set they realised that they were lost. They were tired and exhausted. After some time they reached a place where three roads met.

"Which road shall we take?" said the emperor. "Which do you think goes to Agra?"

All the roads looked the same. The men were confused. Just then, a young man came walking down one of the roads. The emperor's men were really pleased to see the young man. They asked him to come forward. He did so, looking curiously at the royally-dressed hunters.

"Do you know, young man," asked Emperor Akbar "which road goes to Agra?"

The young man smiled and said, "*Huzoor* (sir), everybody knows that roads do not go anywhere. How can these roads go to Agra or anywhere else?" The young man started laughing at his own joke. The emperor's men kept quiet. 'How can this young man joke with the king?' they thought. The men held their breath. They knew the emperor's temper.

"People go from one place to another," the young man continued, not noticing the silence, "roads don't."

"No, they don't," said the emperor and started to laugh. His soldiers also joined him.

"What is your name?" Akbar asked the man.

"Mahesh Das," he said. "What is your name, *Huzoor*?"

The emperor took off a huge emerald ring from his finger and gave it to the young man. "You are speaking to Akbar, the emperor of Hindustan," he said.

"We need brave and courageous young men like you in our court. Bring this ring with you whenever you come, and I shall recognise and remember you. And now, show us the road we must take in order to go to Agra," said the emperor.

Mahesh Das bowed before the king and pointed towards the road. The emperor and his men galloped away, while Mahesh Das looked on till he could no longer see them.

2
Mahesh Das and the Sentry

As time passed, Mahesh Das finished his studies. He decided to go to Agra and meet the emperor. When he came to Agra, he was dazzled by the huge *havelis* of the nobles, the bustling bazaar and the other sights which were new to him, as he had spent all his life in a village.

He had the king's emerald ring with him. It was nearly evening when Mahesh Das arrived at the king's fort.

It was a massive fort on the banks of the river Yamuna. It had huge wooden gates guarded by fierce-looking sentries. The guards had spears in their hands. Important people hurried in and out of the gate.

Mahesh Das felt very small as he went near the gate of the fort.

He then went up to one of the soldiers and said, "I have come to meet the emperor. He has invited me to come to the court."

"Ho!" said the soldier, looking carefully at his dusty feet and simple clothes. "So, the emperor of Hindustan has invited you to his court," said the soldier, mockingly. "He must have invited you to the *Diwan-i-Khas* (the hall of Private Audience), where he meets high-ranking officials!"

A few passers-by stopped to watch.

"Maybe," said Mahesh Das boldly, keeping his voice steady, even though he was very scared. "I have the emperor's ring to prove it." And from his bag he took out the ring which the emperor had given him.

"Oh," said the guard, doubtfully.

"That is no ordinary ring," said a pundit who had stopped to watch, "you had better let the young man go in."

"Okay, I'll let you go in on one condition. When you meet the emperor, he is sure to give you a gift. I'll let you go in only if you promise to give me half of whatever the emperor gives you."

Mahesh Das agreed at once. The guard threatened him, saying, "Don't forget your promise, or I'll make you very sorry."

Mahesh Das nodded. "I won't forget," he said, and walked into the fort. The emperor was in the *Diwan-i-Aam* (the hall of Public Audience).

The walls of the palace were intricately carved and rich carpets adorned the floor. The *Diwan-i-Aam* was full of courtiers dressed in royal robes. The emperor sat on a platform at the far end of the hall.

Bowing low, Mahesh Das made his way towards the throne.

The courtiers whispered to each other in surprise, "Who is this man?"

Now the emperor happened to look up and immediately recognised him. He asked him to come forward.

"I remember you, Mahesh Das," the emperor said. "I am very glad that you have come. Ask for anything that you want and it shall be yours."

"Your Majesty," replied Mahesh Das, "I just want to be given fifty lashes of the whip."

"Is the man crazy?" the courtiers whispered to each other. But the emperor liked his straightforward manner and said, "Before I grant your strange wish, you must tell us why you want such a gift."

"Your Majesty," replied Mahesh Das, "the sentry who guards the fort allowed me into the fort on one condition: that I give him half of the gift that I receive from you. I am ready to bear twenty-five lashes in order to share it with the guard."

Akbar was enraged when he heard this. "Are my subjects kept away by a greedy guard?" he thundered. "Bring him to me."

The guard was brought before the king and was sentenced to the entire fifty lashes, and never again did he try to bully poor people who came to meet the emperor.

The emperor, impressed with the quick wit and intelligence of Mahesh Das, gave him a place in his court. He also conferred the title of Raja Birbal on him. This is how Birbal became a part of Akbar's court.

3
A Matter of Crows

The king's palace had the *Diwan-i-Aam* and the *Diwan-i-Khas*.

Now the *Diwan-i-Khas* was not as large as the *Diwan-i-Aam*, but was beautifully adorned and lavishly furnished. All the courtiers and nobles met here to discuss the matters of the state.

Apart from the matters of the state, the king also discussed other things. Sometimes the king asked questions which his courtiers were unable to answer. But Birbal always had an answer, no matter how strange the question.

One morning, Akbar asked his courtiers, "How many crows are there in all of Agra? It is important that we have this information immediately. And you have to give me the correct answer, or else there will be serious trouble, I warn you."

The courtiers were scared. Some had a reasonable idea of how many elephants there were in the city. Many of them also knew how many horses there were. One of them even knew the number of pet parrots. But nobody knew the number of crows in the city.

The courtiers were in a fix. If they did not answer the king they would be punished, and if they gave the wrong number, then too, they would be punished. Some courtiers began to pray, while some looked at the sky trying to count the crows.

Only Raja Birbal was calm. After some time he said, "Your Majesty, there are exactly ten thousand, six hundred and sixty-six crows in all of Agra."

"Are you sure, Birbal?" asked the emperor. "We shall have the crows counted to make sure the number you have said is correct."

"By all means, Your Majesty," said Birbal, calmly. "But I cannot be sure that all the crows will remain in Agra till the counting is complete. Many may go and visit their friends and relations in Delhi, in which case there will be less than the number I gave you. It is also possible that many relatives and friends of these crows may come to visit them in Agra, and so it will increase the number. But I can surely say that at this moment there are ten thousand, six hundred and sixty-six crows in Agra."

The king burst out laughing and said, "Birbal, you are amazing!"

4
Length of the Stick

There once lived a merchant in Agra. He was very rich. One day, a burglary took place in his house. The merchant suspected one of his servants. But he did not know which one of them was the thief. So he went to Birbal to ask for his help.

Birbal, after hearing the merchant's problem, asked the merchant to take him to his house. At the merchant's house, Birbal called all the servants and spoke to them.

"You all know about the burglary which has taken place. If any one of you has committed the crime, come forward and admit it. I assure you that you will be forgiven." But nobody came forward. They all insisted that they were innocent. Then Birbal gave each servant a stick and asked him to keep it carefully. He said to them, "The sticks given to you are of equal length. They look ordinary, but they have magical powers. The stick kept by the thief will grow two inches longer by tomorrow."

Now the thief was very worried. He could not sleep the whole night. He knew he would get caught the next day as his stick would grow two inches longer. Then an idea struck him. He got up and cut his stick two inches short, thinking that if the stick grew two inches in length, it would remain the same as those of the others.

Next morning, Birbal returned to the merchant's house. He asked all the servants to bring their sticks. After glancing at their sticks, he pulled out one of the servants and said to the merchant, "Here is your thief."

The servant fell at Birbal's feet and asked for forgiveness. The merchant thanked Birbal and asked him if the stick had really grown two inches longer.

Birbal laughed and said, "Oh, those were just ordinary sticks. But the thief was scared that his stick would grow longer, so he cut it and his stick became shorter than the rest. So I looked for the man with the shorter stick."

Birbal's cleverness helped in catching the thief.

5
Half-light, Half-shadow

Once Akbar, in a fit of anger, asked Birbal to leave the city. Birbal agreed, but before leaving, said that he would enter the city only when the emperor asked him to.

Many days passed and Akbar started missing his friend. He found it difficult to pass his time. He wanted Birbal to come back. So he sent his men in search of Birbal. They searched everywhere, but could not find him.

Then the king had an idea. He announced a reward of a thousand gold coins for a man who would come to the court in half-light and half-shadow. The king knew that Birbal would not be able to resist this challenge.

Now Birbal was staying with a brahmin in a small village. He heard of the king's proclamation.

He wanted to return the brahmin's kindness. He asked the brahmin, "Have you heard of the king's proclamation?"

"Yes, I have. But how is it possible to go in half-light and half-shadow?" asked the brahmin.

Birbal said that the brahmin could win the reward if he followed his instructions. He said to the brahmin, "Take a *charpoy* (cot) and enter the palace carrying it on your head. This way you will be half-in-light and half-in-shadow."

So, the brahmin went to the palace carrying the *charpoy* on his head.

The king was very happy and said, "Brahmin, before I give you your reward, tell me if this was your idea or somebody else's."

The brahmin was scared. He said, "A poor brahmin, who has been staying with me for the past few weeks, gave me this idea."

The king knew that this brahmin could be none other than Birbal. He gave the brahmin his reward and sent his men to the brahmin's house to get Birbal back. The king was very glad to have Birbal back again.

6
Who is the Greater Fool?

Once Akbar asked Birbal to make a list of all the fools in Agra. So Birbal searched the streets, looking for fools.

Meanwhile, a merchant from a faraway land arrived at Akbar's court. The king asked the merchant about the purpose of his visit.

"Your Majesty, I sell horses of the finest breed. I have brought one of my horses as a sample. Please see it," said the merchant.

Now Akbar was very fond of horses. He had many in his stables, but he could not resist buying another fine horse. So he went with the merchant to see the horse. "This is really a fine horse," said Akbar.

"Your Majesty, this is only a sample, I have a hundred such horses. Would you like to buy them all?" asked the merchant.

"Yes, I would like to buy all those horses. When can you bring them?" asked the king.

"Your Majesty, I would have brought them, but transporting so many horses requires a lot of money and I didn't have all that money. If you would be kind enough to give me one lakh gold coins, then I could bring the horses in a fortnight," said the merchant.

The king called his treasurer and asked him to give the merchant one lakh gold coins. After taking the gold coins, the merchant left.

Akbar was very happy with himself, thinking that he had struck a good bargain. He showed Birbal the horse. He also told Birbal that he had given the merchant one lakh gold coins, so that the merchant could bring the rest of the horses.

"You mean you have given the merchant so much money in advance?" said Birbal, disbelievingly.

"Yes, the horses are cheap even at that price," said Akbar.

"But Your Majesty, do you have his address, or did someone at the court stand guarantee for him?" asked Birbal.

"No, but he looked very honest. I am sure he will come back. Now you tell me about the list of fools. Have you completed it?" asked Akbar.

"It is almost finished. I just have to add one more name to it," said Birbal. He quickly wrote down a name and gave it to Akbar.

When Akbar saw the list, he was shocked. Even his name was on the list.

"How dare you write my name on the list?" Akbar asked Birbal.

"I beg your pardon, Your Majesty. But you have just given one lakh gold coins to a stranger. What could this be, but an act of foolishness!" said Birbal.

"But what if the merchant returns with the horses after a fortnight?" asked Akbar.

"Then I will strike off your name from the list and write his name instead," said Birbal. Akbar could not help laughing. As usual, Birbal got away with a witty answer.

7
The Most Beautiful Child

King Akbar adored his grandson and would spend hours playing with him. Whenever he would come to the court, he would only talk about his grandson.

"There is no baby as handsome as my grandchild," said Akbar, and all the courtiers agreed with him. They dared not refute the claims of the king.

But Birbal said, "Your Majesty, no doubt the young prince is very good-looking, but all parents find their children very beautiful."

This enraged Akbar. So one of his courtiers suggested that each of them should bring a child whom he thought to be beautiful. Then they could judge who was the most beautiful.

The next day, each of the courtiers brought a child. The king saw each child, but he still insisted that his grandson was the most handsome child. Finally, he came to Birbal.

Birbal did not have any child with him. Akbar asked him why he had not brought a child.

Birbal said, "I have found a child who is the most beautiful child in the whole country. However, the mother refused to let me bring the child to the palace. She did not want strangers to cast their eyes on her child."

"In that case, we will go in disguise and see the child ourselves," said Akbar.

So Akbar and Birbal, accompanied by a few ministers, travelled to the other end of the city. Birbal took them to a small, dirty hut. A child was playing in the sand. His body was covered with dust. Akbar and his ministers were shocked. It was the most ugly-looking child they had ever seen. The child had pox marks on his face, was dirty and had a running nose.

"Birbal, you call this child the most beautiful? This is the ugliest child I have ever seen!" said Akbar.

The mother of the child heard what he had said. She was very angry.

"How dare you call my child ugly! He is the most beautiful child God has given me. Go away!" she screamed, and picked up her baby. She wiped his face and kissed him lovingly. She took her child inside and closed the door.

"You were right, Birbal. To all parents, their children are the most beautiful," said Akbar.

"And also to their grandparents," teased Birbal.

8
The Punishment

Everybody knew that Akbar was very fond of his grandson. One morning, when Akbar was getting ready for the court, his grandson came running to him.

"Grandfather, there is something black in your moustache. Bend down and I will take it out," said his grandson.

As Akbar bent down, his grandson pulled out a hair from his moustache.

"Ouch!" screamed Akbar. "Why did you do such a naughty thing?"

"Ha! Ha! I fooled you!" said his grandson.

"Now go and play, I have to go to the court," he said.

On his way to the court, Akbar thought that he would give all his ministers a problem to solve. When he reached the court, he

addressed his courtiers saying, "Someone pulled a hair from my moustache this morning. I want him to be punished. What punishment should I give him?"

The courtiers were shocked when they heard this. 'How could anybody dare to pull a hair from the emperor's moustache?' they thought. All the courtiers started giving their suggestions.

"The man should be flogged a thousand times," said one courtier.

"He should be imprisoned for life," said another.

"He should be hanged," said somebody.

While everybody was giving suggestions, Birbal kept quiet.

"Why are you so quiet? Don't you have any suggestion, Birbal?" asked Akbar.

"No, that is not the case. Maybe I should tell you in private," said Birbal.

"No, everyone should hear what you have to say," said Akbar.

"The guilty person should be given a kiss," said Birbal.

Everybody was shocked. They thought that Birbal had gone crazy.

"Birbal, can you explain why you suggested such a strange punishment?" asked Akbar.

"Your Majesty, only a child can do such mischief, and that child could only be your grandson," said Birbal.

Akbar and all the other courtiers were full of praise for Birbal's cleverness.

9
Begum and Birbal

Everybody knew that Birbal was the king's favourite. Many courtiers were jealous of him. They always tried to poison the king's mind against him.

Once the courtiers decided that they should remove Birbal from the minister's post and make Hussain Khan, the king's brother-in-law, the minister. So they went to Hussain Khan's house and asked him to be the minister.

"But the emperor will not make me the minister while Birbal is here," said Hussain Khan.

"Why don't you ask your sister (the king's wife) to plead your case with the emperor?" said one of the courtiers.

"That's a good idea. I will go tomorrow to my sister," said Hussain Khan. So the next day, he went to meet his sister and persuaded her to ask the emperor to make him the minister.

When the emperor came, the Begum (queen) said, "I want my brother Hussain Khan to be made the minister in place of Birbal."

The king was surprised at this strange request and said, "How can I do that? I need somebody intelligent to run the affairs of such a vast empire, and nobody is better than Birbal. Moreover, how can I remove Birbal without any valid reason?"

"Give him a tough task to do and when he fails, you can remove him," suggested the Begum.

"In that case it's better that you suggest a task," said the emperor.

"When you are taking a stroll in the palace garden, ask him to fetch me. I will make sure that he does not succeed," said the Begum.

The king agreed, and the next day while taking a stroll in the palace garden, he sent Birbal to fetch the Begum. He also told Birbal that if he failed to bring the Begum with him, he would be removed from his post and Hussain Khan would be appointed in his place.

Birbal realised that his enemies wanted to get rid of him. He thought of a plan. He called one of the messengers and explained his plan to him. Then he went to the Begum's palace and conveyed the message to the queen.

He said, "His Majesty is strolling in the palace garden. He wishes to meet you in the garden."

Just at that moment, a messenger came and said to Birbal, "I have a message for you, *Huzoor*, which I can only tell you in private."

So Birbal excused himself and walked aside to hear the message.

Meanwhile, the Begum was curious to listen to the message. So she tried to overhear what they were saying, but the only words she could hear were, "she is beautiful".

Birbal immediately went to the Begum and said, "The whole situation has changed. You need not come, Begum *Sahiba* (term of respect for lady)." Soon after, Birbal left.

But the Begum became very suspicious. She thought that some beautiful maiden had come to see the emperor, and Birbal did not want her to see both of them together.

She hurried to the palace garden, but was surprised to see the emperor alone.

"So Begum, you have come. You had promised that you would not come," said Akbar.

The Begum repeated what Birbal had said.

"Just because Birbal said the situation had changed, you came running here?" said Akbar.

'How can I tell you that it was the fear of a beautiful maiden that brought me here,' thought the Begum.

Just then Birbal came, and Akbar, on seeing him, said, "Birbal, as usual, this time too, you have won."

10
Those Who Cannot See

Once Akbar was looking at a list of all the blind people in the city. Birbal was also with him.

"Birbal, the Begum wants to give alms to all the blind people, so I asked my men to make a list of all the blind people in the city. I see there are very few blind people."

"But, Your Majesty, those who are blind are more in number than those who can see," said Birbal.

"How can you say that, Birbal? My men made a careful check. They can't be wrong," said Akbar.

"Your Majesty, they forgot to include those who have eyes, but cannot see," said Birbal.

"Birbal, I don't want to hear any of your jokes," said Akbar.

"It is true, Your Majesty. I will prove it to you. Give me just a few days," said Birbal.

Akbar agreed and the next day Birbal went to the marketplace and started weaving a cot. Now everybody around was curious to know what Birbal was doing. So they all came and asked Birbal what he was doing. Birbal did not reply. Instead, he asked his attendants to write down their names. As the word spread around, more and more people came to see Birbal. They all asked him the same question. Birbal did not reply, but wrote down their names.

Soon the news reached Akbar's ears. Even he was curious to know what Birbal was doing. So he went to the marketplace and saw Birbal weaving a cot. He also asked Birbal what he was doing.

Ignoring the emperor, Birbal turned to his attendant saying, "That will be two hundred and fifty."

"Birbal, why don't you answer my question? What are you doing?" asked Akbar, angrily.

"Your Majesty, I am weaving a cot and also making a list of the blind people," said Birbal. "Today two hundred and fifty people asked me what I was doing, though I was working in broad daylight."

Akbar asked Birbal to give him the list. When he saw the list, he was surprised to see his name also in the list.

"But why do you have my name here?" asked Akbar, angrily.

"Because you were the last person to ask me what I was doing," said Birbal. As usual, Birbal had the last word.